# Jim Henson

*From Puppets to Muppets*

# Jim Henson
### From Puppets to Muppets

## by Geraldine Woods

Taking part BOOKS

**dP** DILLON PRESS, INC.
Minneapolis, Minnesota 55415

Acknowledgments

*A special thanks to everyone at Henson Associates—Jim Henson, Louise Gikow, Danielle Obinger, Ruth Gruhin, and Harriet Yassky in particular—for their assistance in the creation of this book. Without their help, this biography of Jim Henson would not have been possible. The photographs are reproduced through the courtesy of Henson Associates, Inc., Christopher Reeve (page 99), Jimmy Dean (page 22), and United Press International/Bettmann Archive (page 48/ bottom).*

Library of Congress Cataloging in Publication Data

Woods, Geraldine.
Jim Henson : from puppets to muppets.

(Taking part)
Includes index.
SUMMARY: Recounts the life story of the puppeteer whose remarkable creations, the Muppets, have found success in television and other media.
1. Henson, Jim—Juvenile literature.   2. Puppeteers—United States—Biography—Juvenile literature.   3. Muppet show (Television program)—Juvenile literature.   4. Television producers and directors—United States—Biography—Juvenile literature. [1. Henson, Jim. 2. Puppeteers.   3. Television producers and directors.   4. Muppet show (Television program)]   I. Title.
PN1982.H46W66   1986      791.5'3'0924 [B] [92]     86-11624
ISBN 0-87518-348-4

Dillon Press, Inc., 242 Portland Avenue South
Minneapolis, Minnesota  55415

Printed in the United States of America

1  2  3  4  5  6  7  8  9  10  96  95  94  93  92  91  90  89  88  87

# CONTENTS

# JIM HENSON

For the past 30 years, Jim Henson's Muppets have entertained and educated millions of people of all ages, especially children. Around the world loyal fans watch TV shows and movies to see his remarkable creations—the familiar and incredibly popular Muppets such as Kermit and Miss Piggy, and the amazing characters brought to life in movies such as *The Dark Crystal* and *Labyrinth.* "Sesame Street," "The Muppet Show," and "Fraggle Rock" have reached a worldwide audience numbering in the hundreds of millions.

Today, despite his wealth and fame, Jim Henson remains a modest, friendly, hard-working and well-liked artist, performer, and family man. Throughout his performing career, beginning with a local TV show in Washington, D.C., Jim Henson has developed and expanded the art of puppetry in the electronic age. Along the way, he has created whole worlds from his imagination that make use of new technology in exciting ways. Jim Henson has gathered a talented group of performers who share his enthusiasm. A number of them have worked with him for many years and have become part of his creative family. But above all, Jim Henson has achieved success in his own way—while having fun.

*Jim Henson with Kermit,*
*the famous Muppet and*
*star of* The Muppet Movie.

# 1/". . .I absolutely loved television."

A small, green frog sits on a log in the middle of a Georgia swamp. As he calmly strums his banjo, cameras record his every move. Beneath the murky water, in a metal tank underneath the frog, a tall, thin man crouches. His right arm is raised above his head. It is covered with a rubber sleeve and the soft cloth of the frog's body. The man moves his hand to make the frog's mouth open and close. His other hand works a stiff wire to pass the frog's arm over the banjo strings. As his hands move, the man watches the frog on the tiny television set between his knees.

Divers stand by to rescue the man in case the tank leaks. Air is pumped in so he can breathe. From time to time, a glass of iced tea is passed to him through the rubber sleeve. It's a long day.

The frog (better known as Kermit the Frog) is the star of *The Muppet Movie*. The swamp scene takes place at the beginning of the film. At that point in the story, Kermit is still an unknown frog. He is about to begin a journey that will take him from his quiet childhood to fame and fortune in show business.

The man in the tank, Jim Henson, knows all about that kind of journey. As a matter of fact, he once took it himself. Along the way, Jim made some award-winning movies and two of the most popular television shows in history. He also created the best known and most popular puppets in the world—the Muppets.

James Maury Henson was born on September 24, 1936, in Greenville, Mississippi. His father, Paul Henson, was a scientist who studied new types of crops that animals could eat. One of his crops was called "birdsfoot trefoil." Years later, his son used the name "Herbert Birdsfoot" for one of the Muppet characters. He also borrowed the first name of a grammar school classmate, Kermit Scott, for his famous frog.

Jim attended grammar school in Leland, Mississippi. Although he says he was only a "medium-good" student, he received excellent grades. His best subject was art, and he always tried to include artwork in his reports and projects for other classes. In his free time, he often painted and drew cartoons just for fun.

Jim also enjoyed his school's plays. In fact, he began his long career in show business in one of these plays, "Parade of Spices." Each student took the part of a different seasoning—pepper, cinnamon, and so forth. Jim took the role of sage, a spice used in turkey stuffing!

After school, Jim played tennis, cards, and board games games with his friends and with his older brother Paul. On his own, he put together a stamp collection.

Jim's family moved to Hyattsville, Maryland, a town near Washington, D.C., when his father's job in Mississippi was completed. Jim attended high school in University Park, Maryland. Again, he was a star in his art courses. However, he recalls that he had a hard time with foreign languages. He also designed the scenery for several school plays, and did a bit of acting. In one mystery drama, *Arsenic and Old Lace*, Jim played a minister.

Like most other young people in those days, Jim enjoyed listening to the radio. Television hadn't been invented yet, but mystery, adventure, and comedy shows were broadcast on the radio every day. The radio provided one of Jim's earliest experiences with puppets. One of his favorite radio shows starred Edgar Bergen and two imaginary characters named Charlie McCarthy and Mortimer Snerd. Charlie and Mortimer were actually dummies—dolls with movable jaws. On the show, Edgar and "Charlie" or "Mortimer" would have a conversation with a famous guest star. On the radio, it was almost impossible to tell that Mortimer and Charlie were not real. Jim once said that the two puppets "were human to me."

Then, around 1950, television came on the scene. Jim was fascinated. "My mother tells me that I badgered the family into buying a television set," he says. "As soon as we got that set I absolutely loved television. I was tremendously excited by [it]."

One television show that was on the air when Jim got his first TV was "Kukla, Fran, and Ollie." On the show a woman named Fran talked with Kukla and Ollie the Dragon. Kukla and Ollie were hand puppets, operated by puppeteer Burr Tillstrom by putting his hands into the puppets' soft bodies. By wiggling fingers and moving his arms, he could make the puppet seem alive. Burr Tillstrom also made up all of Kukla and Ollie's spoken parts for the show—on the spot! There were never any scripts. He just made up everything they did and said.

Jim remembers watching "Kukla, Fran, and Ollie" every evening. He soon joined his high school puppet club. Jim says now that he had no plans at that point in his life to make puppetry his career. In fact, he first wanted to become a cartoonist. Then, after working in his high school plays, he became interested in theater and scene design.

More than anything else, though, Jim wanted to work in television. "As soon as I was old enough to get a job, when I was sixteen, I went out and approached all the little studios in Washington to apply for work.

"In the beginning," continues Jim, "puppetry was merely a way of working on television. When I heard that a local station was looking for a puppeteer, I built some puppets with another young guy and got the job." Jim's job was on a children's program, "The Junior Morning Show." The puppets he used were a French rat named Pierre and some cowboys.

"The Junior Morning Show" lasted only a few weeks. In that short time, Jim received good reviews in several newspapers. Soon, Jim and his puppets were hired by NBC to perform on local programs.

While his new career grew, Jim entered the University of Maryland to study art. One of his courses was in puppetry. In May 1955, at the end of his first year in college, Jim Henson got his big break. WRC-TV, a Washington station, offered Jim his own show. The program was called "Sam and Friends." Jim says it was a "nice little show that was on late at night and. . .was only five minutes long. Nobody attached too much importance to it so we could do almost anything we wanted to."

The star of "Sam and Friends" was a little, bald fellow. In spite of his small size, though, Sam made puppet history. He was neither a puppet nor a marionette. A marionette is a doll with long strings attached to its body. When the puppeteer pulls the strings, the doll's arms, legs, and body move. Sam, in fact, was a

Muppet—a name Jim created especially for his act.

The heads of most puppets are made of wood or other stiff materials. Their mouths and eyes may sometimes be moved up and down or sideways. The puppeteer, however, cannot change the expression on the puppet's face. In a live puppet show, the audience is usually so far away from the stage that they can't see the puppet clearly, anyway. The puppeteer shows a puppet's feelings by moving its body, arms, head, and legs, or by changing its tone of voice.

Television, however, is different. Because the camera can easily shoot close-ups, audiences have a clear view of the puppet's expression. On TV, then, the puppet has to be able to smile, frown, and look puzzled, angry, or shy. That's why most of the Muppets have soft heads. "We would build puppets out of foam rubber, surfacing them with fabric," Jim says. "We used a stretch fabric—a kind of fleecing." By pinching and stretching the Muppet's faces, Jim was able to make his Muppets act out many feelings.

Muppets are also different because they do not perform in a puppet theater, with the puppeteer hidden above or below the stage. Jim came up with the idea of showing only the puppets and the set on the TV screen. That is important because it allows the puppeteers to move freely around the stage below.

The puppeteers don't watch their arms or each other when they work with the Muppets, either. They watch a television monitor. This small TV screen shows them how their characters appear to the audience.

The star Muppet of "Sam and Friends" didn't talk during his performances. He danced and clowned while a record played in the background. As Jim explains, "We very often would take a song and then do strange things to it. . .It was a way of doing entertaining things rather safely and easily."

Jim also remembers that some of the "Sam and Friends" shows were "slightly strange. . .that nobody could quite understand." He adds, "I always enjoyed doing those!" One show starred a puppet made from a squirrel skull that pretended to sing a song called "There's a New Sound." Jim says the song was "terrible—it would just drive everybody crazy."

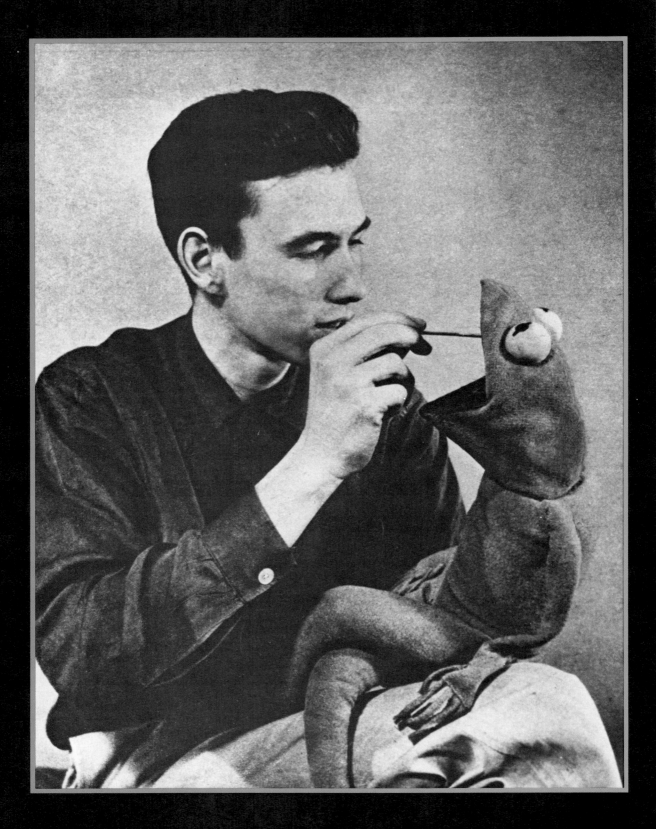

## 2/"Puppetry is putting a mirror up to ourselves."

The Muppets Jim used on "Sam and Friends" were not modeled after any particular animal or person. They were fantastic creatures, born in Jim's imagination. For one Muppet, however, Jim took his mother's old, green spring coat and two Ping-Pong balls. He made a part-lizard, part-frog Muppet—an early Muppet that looked much like Kermit!

After "Sam and Friends" had been on the air for a while, Jim was asked to perform on another show. Busy with "Sam and Friends," the new show, and school, Jim needed help in the TV studio. He asked another student from his puppetry class in college to help him. His new partner, Jane Nebel, soon became a close friend. Jim and Jane worked well together, and "Sam and Friends" stayed on the air for eight years. In 1959 it won a local Emmy award.

Since "Sam and Friends" was a local TV show, the first Kermit was seen only by people in the Washington, D.C./Baltimore area. In 1956, however, Kermit appeared throughout the

*A young Jim Henson fixes Kermit's throat for "Sam and Friends."*

United States for the first time. The occasion was the "Tonight Show." Kermit, wearing a blond wig, sang "I've Grown Accustomed to Your Face" to a purple monster named Yorick. Jim operated Kermit. Jane worked the monster, who ate its own face during the performance and then tried to gobble up Kermit, too.

In 1957 the Muppets began to work in TV advertising. They appeared in a series of commercials for Wilkins coffee. At first Jim and Jane were hired simply as puppeteers. Later they helped direct, produce, and market the ads.

Their commercials were "somewhat revolutionary," says Jim, "because commercials were fairly straight in those days. Ours were among the first funny commercials." In one of their TV ads, a happy Muppet asks a grouchy one what he thinks of Wilkins coffee. The grouch says he has never tried it. The happy character blasts the grouchy one with a cannon, and then aims it at the audience. "What do you think of Wilkins coffee?" he asks. Ads like this one soon became the most popular commercials in Washington, D.C.

In spite of the success of his puppetry, though, Jim still had his sights set on a different career. As he told one reporter, "All the time I was in school I didn't take [puppetry] seriously. I mean, it didn't seem to be the sort of thing a grown man works at for a living."

*Jim Henson created this early Kermit and other Muppets for "Sam and Friends."*

When his college years were over, Jim went on a trip. "I decided to chuck it all and go off to be a painter," he says. Jim spent several months traveling in Germany, Switzerland, Belgium, and England. Although Jane and another friend were now in charge of "Sam and Friends," Jim was still interested in puppetry. In every city he visited the local puppet theater.

Jim was amazed at what he found. In Europe, puppetry is not considered entertainment only for children. People of all ages attend puppet shows. Jim also met many European puppeteers as he traveled. He says, ". . .they were very serious about their work. I thought what they were doing was really interesting." Jim began to realize that puppetry was a true art form and not just a teaching aid for kids.

When Jim returned from his travels, he made two important decisions. He now knew that he wanted to continue working with puppets. As he says, "Puppetry is putting a mirror up to ourselves." In other words, puppets can entertain people just as live actors do. They can show all the feelings and actions that human beings have. When we watch puppets laugh, cry, fight, and make friends, we are really seeing ourselves.

Jim also decided to ask Jane, his business and performing partner, to be his wife. Jane agreed. As she told one writer, "It was admiration at first sight." Jim Henson and Jane Nebel were married in 1959. Lisa Henson, the first of Jim and Jane's five children, was born in 1960. She was followed by Cheryl, Brian, John Paul, and Heather.

During the 1960s, the Muppets were invited guests on many national TV programs. Kermit appeared with Bill Cosby and other well-known TV and movie stars. Rowlf the dog was a regular on "The Jimmy Dean Show" for three years. Each week Rowlf joked with Jimmy, the star of the show, and sang a song with him.

The Muppets were now "talking"—moving their mouths while the puppeteer spoke. They couldn't form every syllable, though. Muppet mouths are so large that they look nervous if they open and close too quickly. To make them appear to speak normally, the human performers had to learn to time the Muppets' mouth movements to match the most important words in each sentence. The performers also had to learn how to be good comedians.

Jim feels that Rowlf's guest appearance helped him improve the Muppets. On "The Jimmy Dean Show" he had a chance to work with some of the best writers and performers in television. "It was wonderful training," he says. "Buddy Arnold was one of the writers and he was an old-fashioned. . .'sock-it-to-'em' joke person. . .You can learn a lot from guys like that."

(Above) *Rowlf appeared with Jimmy Dean on "The Jimmy Dean Show."* (Opposite) *Jerry Juhl joined Jim as a Muppet performer in 1961.*

What can you learn? "You learn to put the funniest word at the end of the line," explains Jim. "You learn to deliver that line really clean and sharp. It's got to be completely clear and understandable. If you stumble over a phrase going into it, you've killed the laugh."

Jane Henson dropped out of the show when the Muppets began to speak. By then, though, other talented puppeteers had begun to join Jim's company. Jerry Juhl, first a performer and

(Above) *Don Sahlin, a talented "Muppet builder," appears with some of the Muppets he helped create.* (Opposite) *Frank Oz, a very special member of the Muppet team, performs Miss Piggy, Animal, Fozzie Bear, and other characters.*

now a writer for the Muppets, arrived in 1961. Don Sahlin, a talented "Muppet builder" who had worked for many years with Burr Tillstrom, came in early 1963. Jim believes that Don Sahlin shaped the way the Muppets now look. He explains that the early Muppets were all very different from each other. Don built Rowlf the dog and many other characters with the same basic Muppet style—a wide, saucer-shaped mouth, round nose, and big eyes.

Another very special member of the Muppet team also joined Jim in 1963. That was Frank Oz, who created Miss Piggy, Animal, Fozzie Bear, and other characters. Jim remembers that Frank Oz "was just a kid of sixteen when I first saw him, but he was already a very talented performer with a sense of timing and a rapport [way] with the audience that was absolutely brilliant." Though Jim admired Frank right away, he had to wait until the young puppeteer grew up before he could hire him! Frank Oz finally began performing with Jim when he was twenty-one years old.

*Jim Henson surrounded
by many of his well-
known Muppet characters.
As the Muppets grew,
Jim began to develop his
interest in moviemaking.*

# 3/"I think life is basically good."

As the Muppets grew, Jim, who never does just one thing at a time, continued to experiment with film. He had been interested in moviemaking for years. During college he had done some "cartooning" by filming some of his paintings. Jim would draw a few strokes, run the camera, draw a little more, film again, and so forth. With this method he could actually see his picture move. He says that from this point on he lost interest in ordinary painting. "The movement. . .was just so much more interesting," he explains.

In 1964 Jim made a film called *Timepiece*. Only ten minutes long, it mixed live action with cartoon scenes. "When I was working on movies like *Timepiece*," says Jim, "I thought of myself as an experimental filmmaker." In this short film, Jim was not trying to tell a story in the usual way. Instead, he was playing with pictures, putting them together in new, interesting patterns.

Jim didn't know if audiences would like *Timepiece*, but that did not worry him. "I always used to think in terms of having two careers going," says Jim, "two threads that I was working on at the same time. One was accepted by the audience and was successful, and that was the Muppets. The other was something I was very interested in and enjoyed." Although he was only trying to please himself, *Timepiece* was praised by many people. It was even named as a candidate for an Academy Award.

Two other Jim Henson films were shown on NBC in the late 1960s. One, *Youth '68*, was named one of the ten best television shows of the year by *Variety*, the show business newspaper. Other television films that Jim made during this period featured the Muppets.

By this time the Muppets were becoming well known across the United States. However, as the 1960s came to an end, their fame took a giant leap. "Sesame Street" went on the air, and *Muppet* became a household word.

Just about every girl and boy in America since then has grown up watching "Sesame Street." Kids know the Muppets Bert and Ernie almost as well as they know their own brothers and sisters.

Jim Henson has been performing Ernie since "Sesame Street" went on the air in 1969. Sesame Street's creator, Joan Ganz Cooney, had been a fan of Jim's for several years before

*Jim Henson and Frank Oz perform the characters Bert and Ernie on the set of "Sesame Street."*

she started work on the children's program. At the time there were few good shows on television for children.

Joan Ganz Cooney set out to create an entertaining but educational program for young people. She planned "Sesame Street" as a kind of nursery school without walls. With real actors, puppets, and cartoons, "Sesame Street" taught numbers, letters, and ideas to kids. Joan Cooney believed the Muppets would help make the program a success.

She was right. From the very first season, the Muppets received more mail than the human actors. Children loved the seven-foot Big Bird, who acts like a small child. Big Bird is operated by Carroll Spinney. He watches a tiny TV set from inside his huge costume to see how Big Bird looks to the audience. Kids also enjoyed Oscar the Grouch's nasty comments and garbage pail, and laughed at Cookie Monster's huge appetite. Both Oscar and Cookie Monster, as well as Grover and Bert, are operated by Frank Oz. Children were especially delighted by "Kermit the Frog of Sesame Street News," Jim's famous character. Besides these stars, new characters are constantly being created for the show. Some have stayed on to become regulars.

Adults appreciated "Sesame Street," too. Jim Henson won two Emmy awards "for outstanding individual achievement in children's programming." Many other groups have honored Jim as well for his work on the show.

Jim wants the Muppets to give young viewers the same message he wants his own children to receive. "As a parent around your children, you behave a certain way. You do positive things that you want them to reflect [show] in their own lives. I feel myself a positive person. I think life is basically good. People are basically good. That's the message I would like to express through the Muppets."

Jim has been careful, though, not to make the Muppet characters perfect "goody-goodies." As children who have watched "Sesame Street" know, Cookie Monster might gobble Ernie's cookies when Ernie is not looking. Bert and Ernie might quarrel about which television program to watch. The mixture of good and bad makes the Muppets seem more real.

# 4/"Kermit is a little snarkier. . ."

Jim was pleased that the Muppets had a starring role on "Sesame Street." But he also worried that the show would make everyone think the Muppets were only for children. Jim had always wanted a wider audience for his program. He explains that "good television . . . works on all levels, children's and adults'."

When Jim went to the television networks with his idea for "The Muppet Show," he wanted a time slot in the evening. That way entire families would be able to watch. However, he was turned down. "The networks . . . didn't think adults would be interested," Jim explains. Luckily, Lord Lew Grade, a British business man, offered Jim a chance to produce "The Muppet Show" in London. Lord Grade planned to sell the show to TV stations around the world.

Jim accepted Lord Grade's offer and, in 1976, "The Muppet Show" went on the air. It was wildly successful. Within three years, the program had an audience of 235 million viewers in

*As Jim Henson and other performers create a scene for "The Muppet Show," a TV monitor shows how the Muppets appear to the audience.*

more than 100 countries. Most importantly, audience surveys showed that Jim was right—of all the show's fans, three out of four were adults.

Each week "The Muppet Show" followed the same pattern. A group of Muppets, including Miss Piggy, Gonzo, Scooter, Rowlf, Fozzie, and Animal, attempted to put on a show. Kermit, the host and leader of the group, tried very hard to organize his pals. This was often difficult, but Kermit never lost his cool. Jerry Juhl, of Jim's company, once said that if "The Muppet Show" were a basketball game, the score would always be Frog 99, Confusion 98.

Many people have compared Jim Henson to the frog he slipped on his arm in time for every show. Jim and Kermit are not completely alike, but they do have some things in common. Like Kermit, Jim is unbelievably patient. He can watch everything almost go to pieces around him and still remain calm. Once, says Jerry Juhl, Jim and the other performers were working on a television special, "Sesame Street," the "Tonight Show," and a big party all in the same week. Jerry said that everyone else was screaming, "How are we ever going to do this?" Jim, on the other hand, was "wandering around in the middle of it all, perfectly calm, perfectly content," according to Jerry. Jim himself said that "Kermit is a little snarkier than I am—slightly wise.

*Jim Henson performs Kermit. Jim and his longtime Muppet friend do have some things in common.*

35

Kermit says things I hold myself back from saying."

On "The Muppet Show," Kermit was respected and loved by his fellow workers. Everyone agrees that this is also true of Jim. Most of his employees stay with him for years and years. Many have become his friends. In fact, visitors to the set where Jim is working are often surprised to see "the boss" skateboarding and flying kites with his crew. Muppet builder Amy Van Gilder sums it up. "Everything about him is special," she says. "Sometimes I think he's from another planet."

On "The Muppet Show," Jim's characters were joined each week by a different human guest star. Singer Elton John, actress Raquel Welch, comedians Lily Tomlin and Bob Hope, and actor Christopher Reeve are just a few of the famous performers who appeared on the show. Edgar Bergen and Charlie McCarthy, whose radio show Jim enjoyed as a child, were on the show during its second year.

The guest stars sang, danced, or traded comedy lines with the Muppets. What was it like to perform next to a bundle of cloth and foam rubber? Lily Tomlin explained to one reporter that the Muppets almost seemed real. The only difference was, as she puts it, "when you break the scene, you don't both go out for coffee. It's sort of sad." Steve Martin, another comedian who appeared on the show, added, "Pretty soon you don't want to

*Actor Christopher Reeve appeared with Miss Piggy and Kermit on "The Muppet Show."*

talk to people anymore. You just want to talk to Muppets."

No new shows were produced after 1981. The program was still popular, but as Jim explained, "I wanted to use our energies to do other kinds of things." During its five seasons, "The Muppet Show" received many awards, including two Emmies.

The Muppets did not retire from show business when their program ended. Reruns of "The Muppet Show" are broadcast in some areas, and "Sesame Street" is still going strong. "Muppet Babies," a cartoon show featuring a very young Kermit and his pals, went on the air in 1984.

The Muppets have also starred in three full-length movies. *The Muppet Movie* explained how Kermit first met Fozzie, Miss Piggy, Gonzo, and his other friends. Human stars Charles Durning, Richard Pryor, Bob Hope, and Dom DeLuise were part of the cast. In 1981 Jim made *The Great Muppet Caper*, the story of the theft of the "Baseball Diamond." Kermit, Fozzie, and Gonzo played newspaper reporters tracking down the scoop on some jewel robberies. Miss Piggy, of course, also had a starring role, along with Diana Rigg and Charles Grodin. Three years later, *The Muppets Take Manhattan* was released. In this film, Miss Piggy married Kermit—but only as part of a Broadway show the Muppets were performing!

The three Muppet films were a great success. After each

*Kermit and Miss Piggy get married in a scene from* The Muppets Take Manhattan.

(Above) *Miss Piggy dances on a nightclub table in* The Great Muppet Caper. (Opposite) *Miss Piggy in the water ballet from the same movie.*

movie, many people wondered why these little cloth and foam rubber creatures proved to be so popular. The characters, Jim says, are a mixture of goodness and innocence. "They represent a positive [good] attitude toward life." Perhaps this adventurous, fun-loving attitude is what attracts so many people to the Muppets.

*In* The Dark Crystal,
*Kira and Jen, two*
*Gelflings—little creatures*
*who look somewhat like*
*elves—travel to a castle*
*with a magic piece of*
*crystal. Along the way the*
*Gelflings meet many*
*fantastic creatures.*

## 5/"Do what you enjoy doing."

"I like creating different worlds of puppet characters," Jim once told a reporter. Jerry Juhl added, "If it's possible with puppets, Henson will probably try it."

These two statements may explain why Jim started a new project, *The Dark Crystal*, in 1982. *The Dark Crystal* was a full-length movie, but the usual Muppet characters did not appear in it. Neither did any human actors.

*The Dark Crystal* presented many new challenges to Jim and his coworkers. The puppets in the film were different from the original Muppets. For one thing, they had arms and legs and often moved through the scenes with their bodies showing—something ordinary Muppets can't do. To achieve this, some of *The Dark Crystal* characters were radio-controlled. Others were skillfully operated by teams of puppeteers hidden under the movie set. Jim had a movable floor built for *The Dark Crystal*. Sections of the floor could be removed to allow puppeteers to hide beneath it while they were moving the characters around.

Probably the hardest job for the film's workers was making the whole project look easy! Jim notes that "in *The Dark Crystal* you see this character walking in the woods, and the audience has no idea that there are television monitors, and cables, and radio control boxes, and all these performers swarming around just out of sight."

*The Dark Crystal* was also a difficult project because Jim and Brian Froud, who helped design the film's sets and characters, had to create an entire world. Jim wrote the story during a blizzard in February 1978. He was snowed in at New York's Kennedy Airport, and he had some time to think and write. In the movie, two Gelflings—little creatures who looked somewhat like elves—had to travel to a castle with a magic piece of crystal. Along the way the Gelflings met many fantastic creatures. They were helped by the Mystics—wise, four-legged beings—and threatened by the Skeksis—dangerous, lizardlike monsters. All these imaginary creatures came to life in the world created by Jim and his skilled company.

Like *The Dark Crystal*, "Fraggle Rock," a cable television show, is also an imaginary world. It is filled with creatures Jim and his helpers made from foam rubber, cloth, and ideas.

Three types of creatures live in Fraggle Rock: Fraggles, the fun-loving, playful characters who are usually at the center of the action; Doozers, little creatures who love to work and spend most of their time building Doozer constructions; and the giant Gorgs, who live outside Fraggle Rock. Each "Fraggle Rock" story tries to show how these different groups must cooperate in order to live together peacefully and happily.

Several methods of moving characters are used in "Fraggle Rock." The Doozers are operated by remote control radio. Performers inside heavy costumes make the Gorgs move. The Fraggles are much like the other Muppets. One of the puppeteer's hands moves the Fraggle's head, and the other controls the Fraggle's arms with wires.

When work on *The Dark Crystal* was completed, Jim began working on a new film, *Labyrinth*. *Labyrinth* starred rock singer David Bowie as the goblin king of a magical world. Actress Jennifer Connelly played a beautiful young girl who has to rescue her baby brother from him.

*Labyrinth*, like all of Jim's work, was filled with amazing puppet creatures. Jim says the *Labyrinth* puppets "stretched all of our skills further than we've ever gone before." At least four puppeteers worked on each character, moving heads, bodies, arms, lips, eyebrows, eyes, and legs. The creatures' skin even had tiny wrinkles and fingerprints!

One of the people working on *Labyrinth* was Cheryl Hen-

(Above) *Brian and Jim Henson perform for the movie* Labyrinth. (Right) *In* Labyrinth *Jennifer Connelly has to rescue her baby brother from the goblin king.*

son, Jim's daughter. Cheryl served as a hand-puppet builder and as a performer for one of the film's creatures. She has worked on a number of her father's projects during the last few years.

Brian Henson, Jim's son, had an important behind-the-scenes job on *Labyrinth*. Brian served as the film's puppeteer coordinator. That meant he was in charge of the army of skilled workers who brought the *Labyrinth* characters to life on the screen. Brian also helped perform Hoggle, the movie's lovable star creature. He dubbed Hoggle's voice and operated some of the electronic controls that produced the expressions on Hoggle's face.

Since he became interested in puppetry and moviemaking, Brian Henson has worked for some well-known film directors. What was it like to work for his father? "On *Labyrinth* we had a very professional relationship," Brian says. "This just happened to work out in such a way that a father got to boss around his son."

Lisa Henson, Jim's oldest child, is also in show business. She is a vice-president at Warner Brothers Studios, a film company. John, Jim's second son, works with a sculptor, a kind of artist. Heather, his youngest child, is still in high school.

At times Jim has had to be away from the family's home in Bedford, New York, for as long as six months. Still, he has found

(Right) *Heather Henson, Jim's youngest child.* (Below) *Jim with his daughter, Lisa Henson, who also works in show business.* (Top, opposite page) *Jane Henson with Kermit and another Muppet.*

ways to stay close to his children. All five of the young Hensons have worked with their dad in television and film.

Though he is a world-famous show business star, Jim keeps his family life private. Jim and Jane Henson have done their best to allow their children to be themselves. The Henson children never had to become Muppet fans. And as each of them has grown older, he or she has made his or her own decisions about a career.

Brian tells what it was like for him: "Because of my father, people say, 'You must have decided to go into the entertainment business when you were twelve.' In fact, at that age, I wanted to play soccer." Brian and Cheryl have chosen to work on some of their father's many projects. And over the years, Jim Henson has been involved in an amazing number of them.

Movies, "Fraggle Rock," "Muppet Babies," and "Sesame Street" have kept Jim incredibly busy. Besides films and TV shows, he has to attend to the business that has grown up around the Muppets. Jim's characters appear in many books and records. They decorate hundreds of toys, sheets, clothes, and even computer software. Jim has so much to do that Dave Goelz, one of the performers, once gave him a diver's weight belt for Christmas. The idea was that the belt would slow Jim down. However, it hasn't worked at all.

Jim usually works on several projects at once because he's a man who looks to the future. No matter what he is doing, his creative mind is always coming up with new ideas, new stories, new characters. In the entertainment industry, though, people work as part of a team. It takes a long time—sometimes several years—to gather all the workers, material, and money needed to produce a movie or a television show.

During those years, Jim creates plans for several other projects! He explains that "by the time I'm actually producing something, part of me is wanting to do something else. I don't particularly want to make my life go crazy doing several things at the same time, but it always seems to happen that way." Jim doesn't seem to mind his busy schedule. "Many people think of work as something to avoid," he once told a reporter. "I think of work as something to seek."

Even the busiest person has to relax sometimes. Jim enjoys traveling, photography, going to the movies, reading, and playing tennis and skiing with his children. He tries to lead a healthy life and doesn't smoke or eat meat.

What's ahead for Jim Henson? He may create more movies and more TV shows, but above all, he will continue to explore new technology and new horizons. "When you get a certain distance through your life," he says, "there are a lot of things you know a lot about. I feel competent [able to do things] in many areas of puppetry, and I feel there's much more that can be done in these areas."

It has been a long road for Jim Henson from "Sam and Friends" to "Sesame Street," the Muppets, *The Dark Crystal*, and *Labyrinth*. Along the way, Jim has created whole worlds from his imagination that have entertained and educated audiences around the world. Most importantly, he has achieved success in a remarkable way—while having fun! Jim has followed the advice he often gives young people who are thinking about their future careers. "Follow your enthusiasm," he says. "It's something I've always believed in. Find those parts of your life you enjoy the most. Do what you enjoy doing."

# INDEX

## ABOUT THE AUTHOR

Geraldine Woods, who often works with her husband Harold, is the author of thirty-five books for young people. She has long been intrigued by Jim Henson because "he created an entire universe out of his imagination, and then found a way to share that universe with people all over the world. Most amazingly, it is obvious that he loves life and enjoys his work. Not many people have achieved that goal!"

Ms. Woods has a special interest in the needs and skills of the students in America's inner cities. She taught remedial reading and writing at Saint Jean Baptiste High School in New York City and currently teaches English at Horace Mann High School, also in New York.